SPORTS GREAT

DAUNTE CULPEPPER

FOOTBALL

SPORTS GREAT TROY AIKMAN
0-89490-593-7/ Macnow

SPORTS GREAT JEROME BETTIS
0-89490-872-3/ Majewski

SPORTS GREAT DAUNTE CULPEPPER
0-7660-2037-1/ Bernstein

SPORTS GREAT JOHN ELWAY
0-89490-282-2/ Fox

SPORTS GREAT BRETT FAVRE
0-7660-1000-7/ Savage

SPORTS GREAT BO JACKSON
0-89490-281-4/ Knapp

SPORTS GREAT JIM KELLY
0-89490-670-4/ Harrington

SPORTS GREAT PEYTON MANNING
0-7660-2033-9/ Wilner

SPORTS GREAT DONOVAN MCNABB
0-7660-2114-9/ Steenkamer

SPORTS GREAT JOE MONTANA
0-89490-371-3/ Kavanagh

SPORTS GREAT JERRY RICE
0-89490-419-1/ Dickey

SPORTS GREAT BARRY SANDERS REVISED EDITION
0-7660-1067-8/ Knapp

SPORTS GREAT DEION SANDERS
0-7660-1068-6/ Macnow

SPORTS GREAT EMMITT SMITH
0-7660-1002-3/ Grabowski

SPORTS GREAT HERSCHEL WALKER
0-89490-207-5/ Benagh

SPORTS GREAT KURT WARNER
0-7660-2034-7/ Rekela

For other *Sports Great* titles call:
(800) 398-2504

DAUNTE CULPEPPER

Ross Bernstein

—SPORTS GREAT BOOKS—

Enslow Publishers, Inc.

40 Industrial Road
Box 398
Berkeley Heights, NJ 07922
USA

PO Box 38
Aldershot
Hants GU12 6BP
UK

http://www.enslow.com

Library of Congress Cataloging-in-Publication Data

Bernstein, Ross.
Sports great Daunte Culpepper / Ross Bernstein.
p. cm. — (Sports great books)
Includes index.
Summary: A biography of the talented quarterback for the Minnesota Vikings who was raised as an adopted child and graduated from the University of Central Florida.
ISBN 0-7660-2037-1
1. Culpepper, Daunte—Juvenile literature. 2. Football players—United States—Biography—Juvenile literature. [1. Culpepper, Daunte. 2. Football players. 3. African Americans—Biography.] I. Title. II. Series.
GV939.C82 B47 2003
796.332'092—dc21

2002152957

Printed in the United States of America

10 9 8 7 6 5 4 3 2 1

To Our Readers:
We have done our best to make sure all Internet Addresses in this book were active and appropriate when we went to press. However, the author and the publisher have no control over and assume no liability for the material available on those Internet sites or on other Web sites they may link to. Any comments or suggestions can be sent by e-mail to comments@enslow.com or to the address on the back cover.

Illustration Credits: All photos © Vincent Muzik except pp. 23, 25, and 28, courtesy Paul Chapman/University of Central Florida.

Cover Illustration: © Vincent Muzik.

Contents

Chapter 1

The Saints Go Marching Home

On January 7, 2001, it was do or die for the Minnesota Vikings. The Vikes, who had started out strong that season by winning their first seven games, had suddenly fallen into a slump. They had lost their last three games and were clearly nursing their wounds as they limped into the playoffs. To make matters worse, Minnesota's star quarterback, Daunte Culpepper, was coming off a serious ankle injury and was not sure whether he would be able to play on the Metrodome's rock hard astroturf. It was there that the Vikings would face the surprising New Orleans Saints and their tenacious sack-happy defense.

The Saints, who had just beaten the heavily favored St. Louis Rams in the NFC Wild Card game, were an up-and-coming force in the NFL. Could Minnesota get past those Saints and make it to their second NFC championship game in just three seasons? The fans were about to find out.

The Vikings hit the field poised and ready to go. Leading that charge was Daunte Culpepper. The second-year quarterback was about to start his first-ever playoff game. Sure, he was the sparkplug that produced the second-highest

Daunte Culpepper looks downfield for an open receiver.

scoring team in the league that season, but would he be ready for the pressure this afternoon?

"It was a huge game for us," said Culpepper. "I just knew that our fans really wanted this one and I didn't want to let them down."

The Vikings got the ball first, and on just the third offensive play of the game, Culpepper hooked up with wide receiver Randy Moss. Moss, arguably the fastest man in the NFL, then sped 53 yards between double coverage and into the end zone to make it 7–0.

After the two teams exchanged field goals, the scoreboard read 10–3 in favor of Minnesota after the first quarter. In the second quarter Culpepper once again showed why he was named as the Pro Bowl starter that season when he hit wide receiver Cris Carter on a beautiful 17-yard touchdown pass. The TD capped a seven-play, 73-yard drive to make it 17–3 at halftime.

Culpepper was unstoppable. At six-foot-four and 265 pounds, would-be defenders bounced off of him like gnats as he scrambled at will throughout the Saints secondary. He was big, fast, and strong—a rare combination of traits.

During halftime, Vikings head coach Dennis Green told his players not to let up. He knew that his team was looking good but he wanted them to stay focused. Culpepper responded by coming out and hitting Randy Moss on an unbelievable 68-yard touchdown bomb just three plays into the third quarter to give Minnesota a commanding 24–3 lead.

New Orleans responded, however. Their young quarterback, Aaron Brooks, threw for a quick TD to Dave Stachelski to start a rally. The Vikes remained calm and answered back by driving down to set up another field goal. Leading the way was Culpepper, who made a key 30-yard scramble to keep the drive alive.

From there it was all Minnesota as Culpepper led the team on a series of fourth quarter drives that took the wind

Culpepper gives a thumbs-up to his teammates on defense while he watches from the sidelines.

out of the Saints' sails. The final blow came when Vikings running back Robert Smith pounced over the goal line for one final touchdown to put the game out of reach. The Saints added a TD late but wound up on the losing end of a 34–16 score. It was an incredible win and the home crowd was thrilled with the results. After the game the players were amazed at Culpepper's performance.

"It was unbelievable for him to do what he was able to do on a sprained ankle," said Carter, who had eight receptions for 120 yards.

Culpepper, who threw for 302 yards and a trio of touchdowns in his first playoff appearance, showed no sign of nerves and was now just sixty minutes away from going to the Super Bowl. Determined, he would work hard that week in preparation for the upcoming NFC Championship game against the New York Giants.

"That game was just huge," Culpepper later said of the Saints game. "Just knowing that we had won and [being] one game away from the Super Bowl was an amazing feeling. You can't duplicate that feeling. I mean to see 65,000 screaming fans just going crazy in the Dome was awesome and something I will never forget. As the clock ticked down I just got goose bumps thinking about how close we were."

Minnesota, losers of four previous Super Bowls, was eager to get back to the big dance. After all, it was just two years earlier that the Vikings had lost the NFC Championship game to Atlanta, 30–27, in an overtime heart-breaker. Culpepper knew that the fans wanted to win badly and he was going to do everything he could to finally get his club to the Super Bowl.

Chapter 2

Growing Up

Born on January 28, 1977, Daunte Culpepper grew up in the small northern Florida town of Ocala, which is located about an hour north of sunny Orlando. His childhood was unlike that of most other kids. Daunte's birth mother is Barbara Henderson. She was serving time in a Miami prison for armed robbery when she gave birth to Daunte. She decided she would give up Daunte for adoption with the hopes that he would get a better life than she could offer him at that time. So, she turned to Emma Culpepper. Emma and she had become friends a few years before while she was in juvenile detention and she knew that she could trust her to raise her baby.

At sixty-two years of age, Emma was well-known in those parts as a real-life saint. She had already raised fourteen other adopted children up to that point of her life. She relied on discipline and faith to provide a solid moral foundation for her kids, and each of them grew up in a safe, loving home.

But by now this woman was widowed and nearing retirement. She wondered if she would be able to keep up with the demands of raising yet another child, much less a newborn infant. But her faith and love of children won out in the end. Daunte became her fifteenth adopted child. Little did she know, however, as she went to pick up this homeless baby, that one day he would pay her back for all of her years of hard work and sacrifice.

Before long Daunte began to thrive in his new environment. His adoptive mother and extended family of cousins were there to help see him through the trials of life. He loved them and was growing up fast. Then, one day he got a phone call from his mother. She told him that she had been released from prison and that she wanted him to come back and live with her. Daunte was not sure what to do. He had been with Emma for more than five years and was happy. He wanted to give his mother another chance though, so he packed up and moved in with her. But after just a week, they both agreed that it would be best for Daunte to move back with Emma. He had become attached to her and his mother did not want to disrupt his life.

Sports quickly became Daunte's favorite thing to do. "Whatever season it was, that was my favorite sport," Culpepper would later say. "Whether it was football in the Fall, basketball in the Winter, or baseball in the Spring, I just enjoyed the competition. I couldn't wait to come home from school as a kid and run out to play ball with my friends. We had so much fun just playing and learning about life through sports."

Daunte realized that he had a real athletic gift but he also wanted to be well-rounded. So he also learned to play the violin as a youngster, showing that he had an artistic knack as well.

Daunte started playing pee-wee football and had moved up the ranks to play organized ball by the seventh grade, where he emerged as a wide receiver. During his first week of practice, however, the team's quarterback threw him a pass that flew over his head and bounced 30 yards downfield. Daunte ran it down, picked it up, and calmly threw it back to the quarterback on the fly. His coach immediately knew that Daunte was going to be his new quarterback. It has been his position ever since.

By the time Daunte got to high school, he was already being talked about by the varsity coaches. He was big, fast, and hungry to win. It was not long before Daunte started to make a name for himself as one of the area's best all-around athletes, competing in football, basketball, baseball, and even weightlifting. He soon realized that he might be able to obtain a college scholarship if he worked hard and stayed out of trouble.

By his junior year at Ocala's Vanguard High School, college recruiters were everywhere, trying to convince Daunte that their school would be the best for him. There was one problem, though. Daunte had poor grades. Sure, he was the "Big Man on Campus," but he was having too much fun and not keeping up with his studies. His GPA was just 1.5, not good enough to get into college. So, despite being one of the most sought after prep recruits in the country for football, basketball, and baseball, many of the nation's premier colleges, including Florida and Florida State, stopped recruiting him when they found out that he might not be able to meet their school's academic requirements for admission. Many simply gave up on him.

Daunte got depressed. He knew that he was not dumb, he just was not working up to his potential. That is when one of the local recruiters from the nearby University of Central Florida, in Orlando, devised a plan to help Daunte bring up his GPA and still get that college scholarship he so desperately wanted. Daunte knew that Emma did not have the money to send him off to school, so he was willing to do just about anything.

Just how badly did this senior-to-be want to show those recruiters that he had what it took to get into college? So badly that he decided to go back and re-take several of his

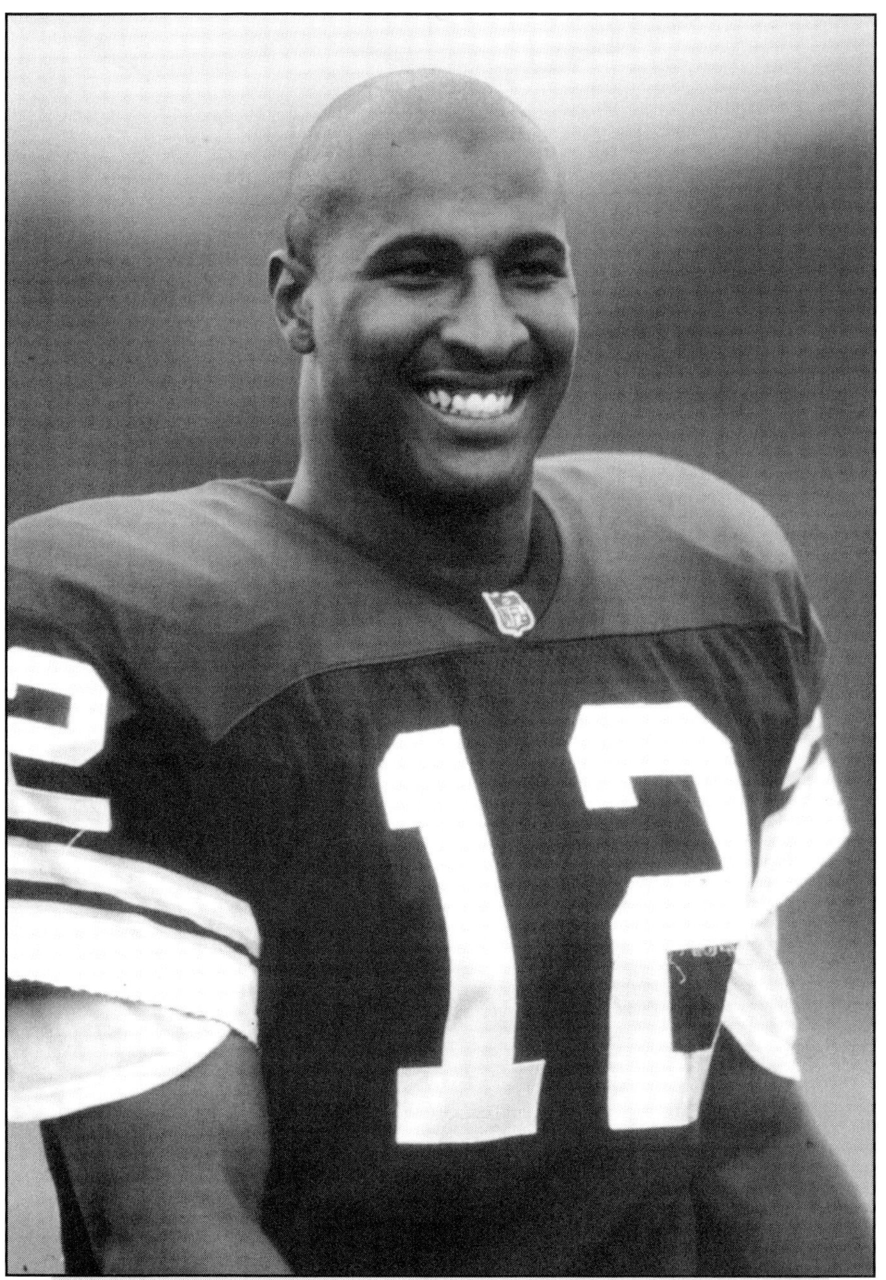

Daunte Culpepper excelled at several sports growing up and also learned to play the violin.

freshman classes over again. And, because he couldn't take them during summer school, he had to sit in with the freshmen all year long.

"It was one of the most humiliating things I have ever had to do," said Culpepper. "I mean I was the man on campus at that time, so that was tough. But it taught me a lot and let me prove that I wasn't dumb or anything. You see, I wasn't a bad kid. Up until that point I had done just enough to get by and remain eligible to play sports. But college was a different story, and I had a lot of growing up to do."

So that year Daunte Culpepper set out to get his grades up and lead his teams to victory. In football, his favorite sport, Culpepper kicked off the season in style by leading his team to a 43–0 victory in the season opener against nearby Leesburg. In that game he tossed four touchdown passes—three of them going to his favorite receiver, Kenny Clark, who also happened to be his cousin.

Culpepper passed for 3,074 yards with 31 touchdowns and rushed for 602 yards that year, earning All-America honors and the prestigious title of "Mr. Football" by the Florida Athletic Coaches Association. In the process he led his Green Knights to an undefeated regular season and to the 1995 Class 5-A state championship game against Bradenton Southeast.

Florida is a football-crazy state. More than 20,000 fans showed up to watch a pair of future NFL stars go at it in the big game: Daunte Culpepper and Peter Warrick (now a wide receiver with the Cincinnati Bengals). Culpepper's stature grew even greater in that game, thanks to an unbelievable scramble for a first down on a dramatic fourth-and-twenty play on the game's final drive. The team missed a last-second field goal, however, which gave rival Bradenton Southeast a 19–17 victory. The missed field goal ended Culpepper's prep career, but he took it in stride.

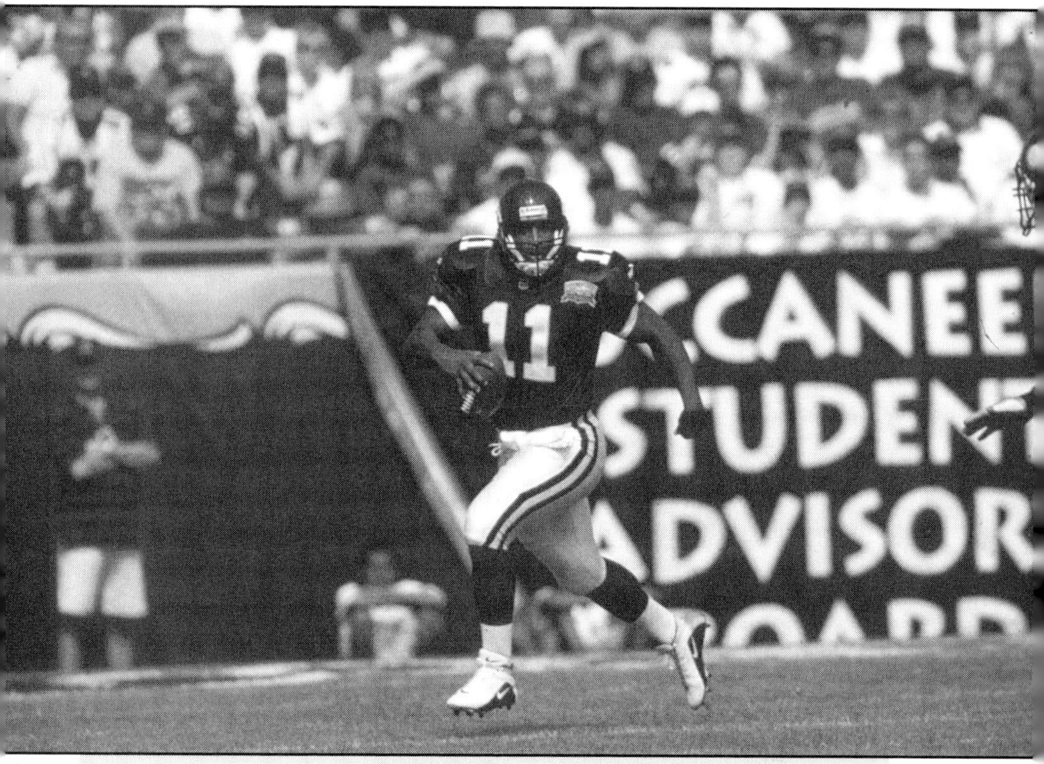

In his senior year of high school, Daunte Culpepper led the school football team to an undefeated regular season and a near-upset in the state championship game.

"Bradenton was the No. 1 team in the nation at the time so we knew it was going to be a battle," said Culpepper. "They had like 15 Division I college recruits and we had like seven, so it was an amazing game with a lot of talent on both sides. We had not been behind at any point during that season though, so to lose was tough. They just jumped out to an early lead and hung on to beat us."

That season Culpepper set the school record for career passing with 6,107 yards and 57 touchdowns in three seasons. He also rushed for 927 yards and 26 more touchdowns. But would he be able to get his grades up to the point where he would be eligible for college? He had already passed his ACT tests, or college entrance exams, but he still had to get his GPA up to a level of 2.0. If worse came to worst, he could always go to a junior college for a year or two until his grades got up to a point where he would be able to transfer. But Culpepper wanted to go to a four-year college right away and show the world that he could do it.

That winter Culpepper lit up the hardwood by averaging 19.5 points, 11.3 rebounds, 5.1 assists, and 3.3 steals per game for his basketball team. He was even being recruited by several major college basketball powerhouses, including the University of Kentucky. Then, in the spring, he tore up the baseball diamond by hitting nearly .500. He was so good in baseball that the six-foot-four, 250-pounder was even selected by the mighty New York Yankees in the 26th round of the Major League Baseball Draft. Culpepper had a lot of options at that point, but he was set on playing college football.

As the school year ended, Culpepper's plan had finally worked itself out. His grades were up to an impressive 3.0 that year and just like that, all of those colleges that had ignored him earlier in the year suddenly started calling again. Nearly every major university in the nation wanted him, but Culpepper was particularly grateful to the University of Central Florida, which had stuck with him through thick and thin. As a result, he snubbed the traditional football powers and rewarded the UCF coaching staff's loyalty and commitment by signing on to play with them. At the time, UCF was nothing more than an average I-AA football program, a division lower than that of the larger schools such as the University of Florida and Florida State. But with Culpepper steering the ship, that was all about to change.

"They really helped me to get my act together in high school," said Culpepper, "so I wanted to reward them and pay them back. I was loyal to them because they were honest and true to me."

The coaches at UCF told Culpepper that he could participate in basketball and baseball as well, but he opted instead to focus on what he thought was his best sport: football. He also knew that he was going to have to work extra hard to get noticed by the NFL scouts at a small school that never played any of its games on national TV. He knew it was going to be a tough battle, but he was ready for the challenge.

"I decided to just play one sport even though I could've played all three," he said. "I just thought that it would be too tough to try and do that. I mean I have to give 110% out there or I am not satisfied, and I didn't want to let my teammates down by being overextended or anything. So, I chose football and the rest is history."

Chapter 3

University of Central Florida

After graduating from high school, Culpepper moved south, to Orlando, where he quickly found himself gearing up to play college football for the UCF Golden Knights. The transition to college was pretty smooth for him, but he knew that it was going to be a big adjustment being away from home.

"I missed my mom at first," said Culpepper. "But I was ready to take the next step in becoming a man. UCF was a great opportunity for me to play football as well as get a great education."

Culpepper jumped right in at UCF and began to learn the offensive system under the tutelage of the team's head coach, Gene McDowell. He lived up to all the advance billing and preseason hype by being named as the starter on opening night. There, despite being sacked on the first play from scrimmage, he showed great poise by completing his first 12 passes en route to upsetting a fifth-ranked Eastern Kentucky squad, 40–32. Culpepper displayed the poise of a veteran that night, finishing 20 of 25 for 254 yards and throwing for three touchdowns.

For his efforts he was named as the Sports Network's I-AA Offensive Player of the Week. So impressive was

Culpepper that he even caught the attention of Pro Football Hall of Fame Quarterback Joe Namath, who just happened to be watching the game on TV. The next day, on Pete Rose's national radio call-in show, Namath compared Culpepper to future Hall-of-Fame quarterback Dan Marino.

The following week, Culpepper threw for 307 yards on 22 of 30 passing against visiting Carson-Newman. Things were looking good for Culpepper, and they got even better three weeks later when he set a school record for completion percentage in a game (.875), completing 14 of 16 attempts for 184 yards and three touchdowns in a 41–14 victory over Samford. He then completed 26 of 38 passes for 252 yards and rushed for one touchdown in a 45–14 loss at Hawaii and finished the season strong with a 184-yard, two touchdown performance in a 37–17 victory over Maine.

By the end of the season Culpepper had truly emerged. With his size, he was built more like a linebacker than a quarterback. Sports fans from coast to coast suddenly became enamored with this gentle giant. He had become the subject of numerous feature stories in the press and even landed on the front page of *The New York Times* sports section. The media attention was, at times, a bit overwhelming.

"I can still remember the post-game of my first-ever game at college during my freshman year," said Culpepper. "Up until that point I had never done a live TV interview, only stuff with newspaper and radio reporters. So, after the big game, which we won, all the cameras just rushed me and nearly knocked me over. I wasn't ready for it and was kind of in shock."

Culpepper's stats were impressive. Despite losing his two best wide receivers to injury (Rufus Hall and Todd Cleveland), he still managed to complete 168 of 294 passes for 2,071 yards with 12 touchdowns. His 2,071 passing yards were the sixth-best single-season total in school history and the most ever by a freshman. He also rushed for five touchdowns and was named as the team's Most Outstanding Offensive Rookie. For his efforts he was named as a third-team All-American, the Freshman Offensive Player of the Year by *The Poor Man's Guide to the NFL Draft*, and was awarded All-Freshman honors by *College & Pro Football News Weekly*.

Coming into the next season Culpepper was tabbed as a preseason All-America selection and was named as *The NFL Draft Report*'s Premier Sophomore in the Nation. Now, with a marquee player leading the way, UCF made the jump to play its first season at the I-A level. Culpepper would finally have an opportunity to showcase his talents in front of the bigger schools throughout America.

Culpepper did not disappoint. The Golden Knights opened the season in grand style by beating William & Mary in a dramatic 39–33 come-from-behind victory. Culpepper twice kept drives alive with clutch third-down scrambles and once with a fourth-down keeper to seal the deal. He finished the game with 307 yards and three touchdowns to start the season on the right foot.

From there UCF kept on rolling, despite the fact that Culpepper sprained his ankle in the second game of the season. He played on and off for the next couple of weeks despite suffering yet another injury, a separated shoulder, early in the second quarter of the Georgia Tech game in Week Seven. In UCF's 42–15 homecoming win against Illinois State, Culpepper passed for 260 yards and a pair of touchdowns. Then, the following week at the University of Alabama-Birmingham, he completed 24 of 36 passes for 421 yards. In addition to running for a score, he tossed three touchdown passes in UCF's 35–13 victory. Culpepper closed out the season by throwing for 327 yards and three touchdowns against Bowling Green, giving him his fourth career game with more than 300 yards passing.

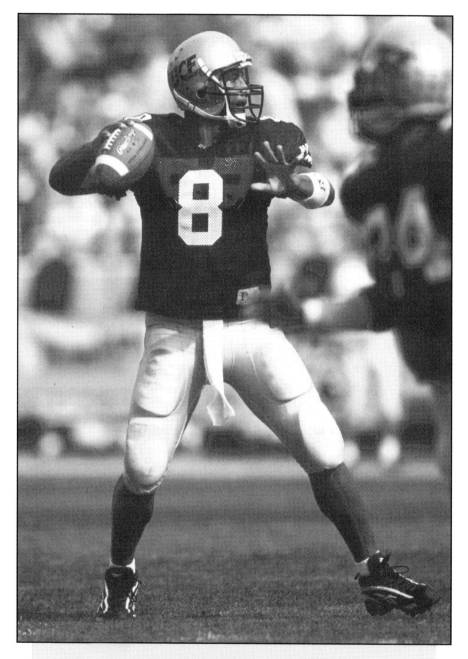

As he entered his sophomore season at the University of Central Florida, Daunte Culpepper was tabbed as an All-American.

For the year Culpepper threw for more than 2,500 yards, despite missing 10 quarters of action due to his ankle and shoulder injuries. He completed 187 of 314 passes for 2,565 yards with 19 touchdowns on the year and was named UCF's Offensive MVP. Things were looking good for the young quarterback. He was once again the "Big Man on Campus" and more and more pro scouts were showing up to watch his games.

The 1997 season would be a record-setting one for the junior quarterback. Culpepper kicked off the year by tossing three touchdowns each against both Mississippi and South Carolina. Then, in a 59–43 win at Kent, he amassed nearly 400 yards of total offense en route to garnering College Football Player of the Week honors. Not only did he complete four touchdown passes, but he also scored on a 75-yard quarterback draw—the longest run ever in school history by a quarterback. For UCF's first home game, against Idaho, a record 41,827 fans filled the team's home Citrus Bowl and cheered Culpepper on to a 41–10 victory. The team was on the rise.

Against Mississippi State he rolled up 420 total yards. The next week, against Northeast Louisiana, he accounted for a school-record 480 yards of total offense, passing for 385 yards and five touchdowns and running for another 95 yards—including a 44-yard touchdown. Perhaps Culpepper's biggest game that season, however, came against mighty Nebraska, when he completed 24 of 35 passes for 318 yards and a touchdown. Culpepper also carried the ball 13 times for 34 yards and a touchdown against the then sixth-ranked Cornhuskers. Culpepper's Knights led three times in the first half, including 17–14 at the intermission, before ultimately falling 38–24. The team finished with a 5–6 record that year. Culpepper knew they could do better.

Still, with fifteen new school records under his belt, it was yet another brilliant season for Culpepper. He passed for

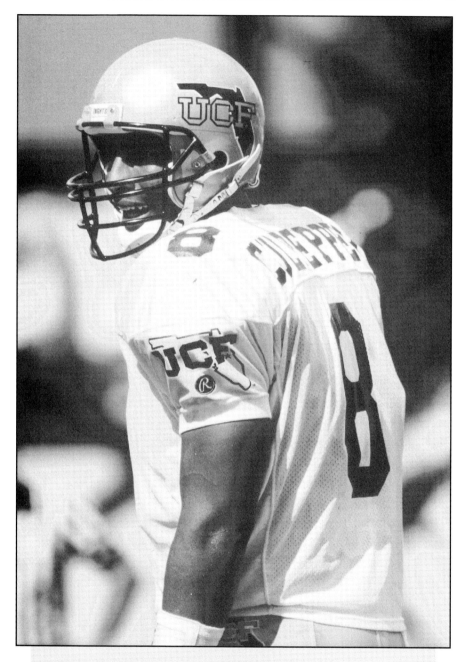

By the end of his junior season, Daunte Culpepper had established fifteen new school records for football at UCF.

3,086 yards on the year, rushed for 438 yards and five touchdowns, and finished with an amazing 3,524 yards of total offense. Culpepper's many honors included being named as a finalist for the Davey O'Brien Award (presented to the nation's best quarterback); a semifinalist for the *Football News* Offensive Player of the Year; a first-team All-American by the *NFL Draft Report*; and being rated as the nation's premier quarterback and second-best offensive prospect (behind Marshall University's star wide receiver, Randy Moss) by *The Poor Man's Guide to the NFL Draft*.

With everything going so well for the young quarterback, many speculated that he might not return to the field for his senior year. He knew that as a first round pick in the upcoming NFL draft, he would become a multi-millionaire overnight. With all of that money he could take care of his mother, Emma, who had worked so hard to raise him. But Emma wanted no part of that and insisted that her son finish what he set out to accomplish, and that was to get his college degree. Culpepper thought about it and agreed. He owed it to UCF to finish out his last year and he owed it to himself to get his diploma.

Head Coach Gene McDowell resigned after that 1997 season and longtime offensive coordinator Mike Kruczek was named to replace him. Kruczek, who had starred as a quarterback for Boston College back in the 1970s before going on to play on two Super Bowl teams with the Pittsburgh Steelers, knew that he could help Culpepper to prepare for the NFL. The team had a new sense of urgency under Kruczek, and Culpepper wanted to make the most of it.

"When I saw Daunte in high school, I couldn't believe it," said Kruczek. "I said, 'No way he's coming to our school.' This was a six-foot-four, 238-pound guy throwing it 40 yards on one knee and running past defensive backs. He's the best I've ever seen, and I played with Terry

Bradshaw. I saw Dan Marino in high school. I know this sounds crazy, but I think he's going to one day be in the Hall of Fame."

The signal-caller's much anticipated senior season got underway with a six-touchdown performance (four passing and two rushing) in a convincing 64–30 win at Louisiana Tech. This was followed by a seven-touchdown encore in a 48–0 drubbing of Eastern Illinois in Week Two, which earned him *USA Today* Player of the Week honors. That next week UCF made its first national television appearance when ESPN televised its game at Purdue. The team came up empty on three first-half attempts inside the Boilermaker 20-yard line, though, and ended up on the losing side of a 35–7 contest.

From there the Golden Knights strung together five consecutive wins for their best start in school history at 7–1. Along the way, Culpepper passed Darin Hinshaw as UCF's all-time passing leader. Culpepper was looking as poised as ever in leading his team. They hit a bump in the road at Auburn, losing a 10–6 heartbreaker in the game's final seconds, but rebounded to finish strong. They won their last two games in style, including a 38–6 triumph against New Mexico in the finale, to finish with their best-ever record of 9–2. After that home season finale against New Mexico, Culpepper showed his appreciation to the fans by grabbing the microphone for the Citrus Bowl stadium's P.A. system and thanking them for four great years.

With that, the Golden Knights accepted a conditional bid to play in the Oahu Bowl in Hawaii. But that post-season highlight was squashed just days later when UCLA was upset by Miami, forcing the bowl selection committee to instead take a team from the PAC-10 Conference to fill the opening. UCF was bounced out of a bowl appearance by a technicality.

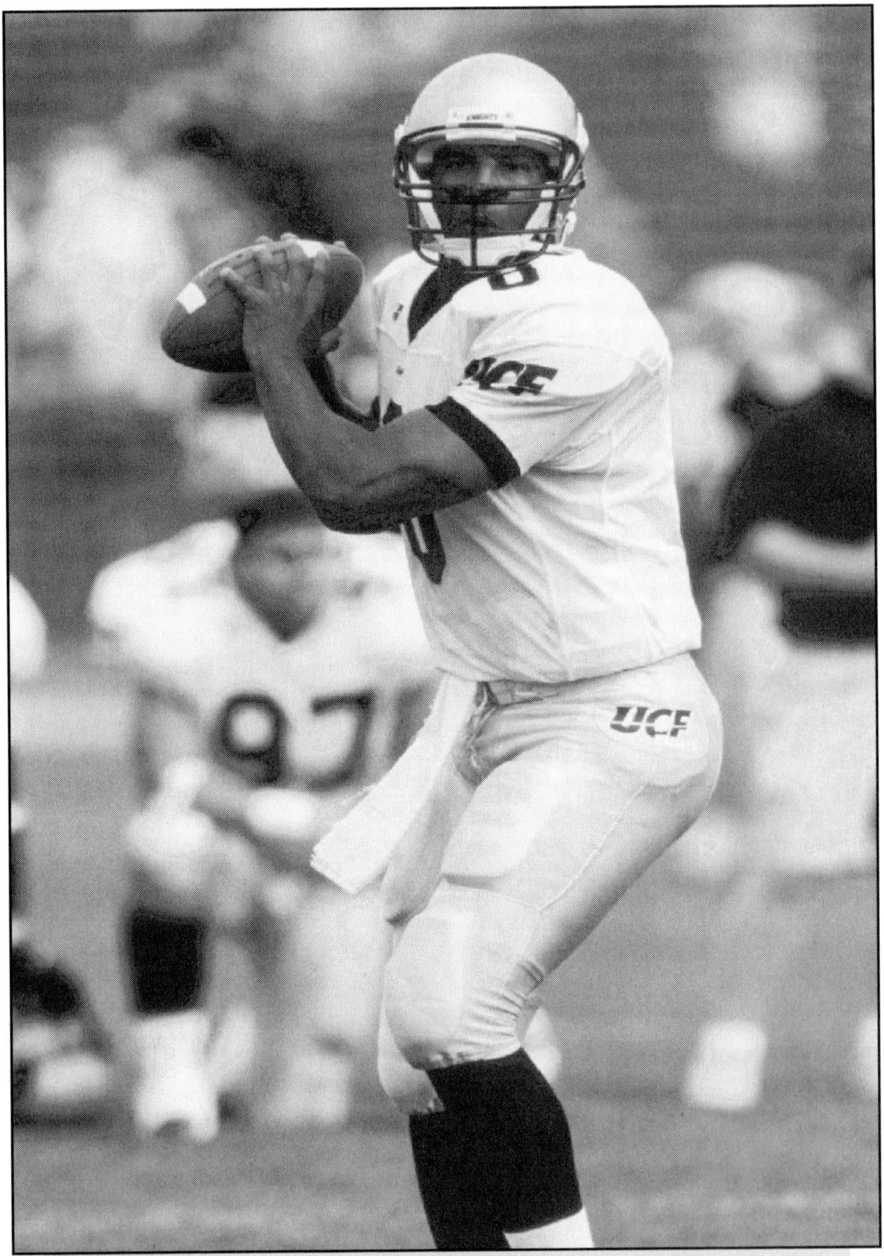

In his senior season, Daunte Culpepper broke the single-season college record for completion percentage by completing 73.6 percent of his passes.

Despite not being able to play in a bowl game, Culpepper was proud of his accomplishments. After all, it was a record-breaking season for the young QB, who broke future Hall of Fame Quarterback Steve Young's 1983 single-season completion percentage record of 71.3 (for Brigham Young University) by completing 73.6 percent of his passes. Culpepper finished the year by completing 296 of 402 passes for 3,690 yards and 28 touchdowns with only seven interceptions. He also carried the ball 141 times for 463 yards and 12 touchdowns. He even became the state of Florida's all-time leader in total offense, topping the University of Florida's Heisman-winning quarterback, Danny Wuerffel, who tossed for 10,500 yards from 1993–96.

Culpepper's stats were simply mind boggling. Overall, he ended his amazing career at UCF with more than thirty school records to his credit and became the first Golden Knights football player to ever have his jersey retired. He became just the third player in NCAA history to pass for more than 10,000 yards and rush for more than 1,000 yards in a career. From there Culpepper went on to finish sixth in the Heisman Trophy balloting and was named national Co-Player of the Year by the Sports Network, along with Texas running back and eventual Heisman winner, Ricky Williams. Other honors included being named as a first team All-American by the *Sports Network and NFL Draft Report*; recipient of the Sammy Baugh Award as college football's Passer of the Year; finalist for the Johnny Unitas Golden Arm Award; and semifinalist for the Davey O'Brien Award.

Despite not being able to play in a bowl game that year, Culpepper did get invited to play in a number of postseason All-Star games, including the Senior Bowl, Hula Bowl, East-West Shrine Game, Blue-Gray Game, and the All-Star Gridiron Classic. The All-Star Gridiron Classic, which pitted Florida's top college players against an all-star team of seniors from the top teams around the country, was his favorite. The game was played in the Citrus Bowl, and his home field fans came out in droves to see him off in style. Culpepper did not disappoint either, racking up big numbers en route to being named as the game's MVP. He even made a curtain call at the end of the game, coming in for one final appearance to let the crowd say goodbye. The stadium erupted in applause when he came out and it was a fitting goodbye to their biggest hero. He had hung in there with them through it all and turned their program into an emerging college football power.

Culpepper was now closer than ever to fulfilling his life-long dream of playing in the NFL. He was just a few classes short of receiving his Bachelor of Arts degree in secondary education, he had made the Dean's list for academic achievement, and he had single-handedly rewritten UCF's record books. He had it all going for him, but he knew that he was going to have to work hard to get ready for the draft.

"After my last game I was really happy," said Culpepper. "I felt like I had done all I had set out to do. Sure, we didn't get to a bowl game, and that was unfortunate, but we came so far as a team. For me it was all about winning as a team and not so much about the records and awards. . . . All in all it was a great run at UCF and I can't thank them enough for taking a chance on me."

Chapter 4

The NFL

Shortly after the end of his senior season, Culpepper began working out diligently to prepare himself for the upcoming NFL draft. The scouting reports on him raved about his poise and leadership. He was seen as a strong-armed quarterback with all the tools to become a star in the NFL. He could run the 40-yard dash in just 4.42 seconds (faster than a lot of wide receivers and cornerbacks—players he outweighed by as much as seventy-five pounds!). He had a thirty-six-inch vertical leap, and he could throw the ball an incredible 80 yards. He could also bench press over 400 pounds and squat 500—more than many offensive linemen. They also said that in addition to being very adept at reading defensive coverages and changing plays at the line of scrimmage, Culpepper also had an uncanny ability to scramble, despite his large frame.

The only problem was that Culpepper had played at a smaller, lesser known college. The scouts and recruiters did not get a chance to see his talents every Saturday on TV like the other kids who played for bigger, marquee programs. They also questioned whether he would be able to handle the complex offensive schemes and defenses that were quicker and more intense at this level of competition. They knew he could dominate at the college level, but they were not totally convinced that he could handle the much bigger and faster professionals.

Culpepper did not care. He went into the pre-draft combines and workouts with a lot of confidence. The teams broke him down every way possible: arm strength, muscle, mobility, intelligence, confidence, maturity, and even the size of his heart. They all came away very impressed. They loved the fact that he was big and strong. With the defensive players getting bigger, faster, and stronger each year, they thought that Culpepper's size would help him to ward off injuries that might otherwise sideline a smaller quarterback.

"He can take hits and stay on his feet to deliver the ball," said Pittsburgh Steelers college personnel coordinator Max McCartney. "He has the perfect combination of strength, mobility and ability. He's a powerful, powerful player."

Things were looking good just prior to the draft, but there were several other big-name quarterbacks entering the draft that year and most of them had played at big-name colleges, in the limelight of the national media. Culpepper remained confident that he would be drafted in the first round, but he did not know where or by whom. All Culpepper could do was to put on his best new suit, fly to New York for the draft, and hope for the best.

There, Culpepper and his agent waited patiently as the NFL Commissioner, Paul Tagliabue, called out the first picks of the 1999 draft. Sitting there with Culpepper was Emma, who had taken her first-ever airplane flight to be there to support her son. Kentucky QB Tim Couch went first, to the Cleveland Browns. He was followed by Syracuse's Donovan McNabb, who went to Philadelphia. Then Oregon's Akili Smith was taken by Cincinnati. Other great players, including running backs Edgerrin James and Ricky Williams, also went high in the draft.

As the 1999 NFL Draft approached, Daunte Culpepper was confident he would be picked in the first round.

Culpepper was feeling somewhat nervous as the No. 10 pick in the draft approached. That's when the Baltimore Ravens selected All-American defensive back Chris McAlister. Down but not out, Culpepper hung in there as Paul Tagliabue calmly approached the microphone and announced that with the No. 11 pick in the draft, the Minnesota Vikings had selected University of Central Florida quarterback, Daunte Culpepper.

"I saw him on TV, the first time," said Vikings Head Coach Dennis Green, "when he was a senior at Central Florida, playing Purdue. I loved everything about him. I loved his poise. I loved the fact that he's a classic drop-back passer, even though he can run. I loved how competitive he was and how he's got that spark, how he makes things happen. As I watched that game, it came to me that Daunte represents the new generation [of] Quarterbacks [who are] bigger and more athletic, and he is leading the way."

Culpepper's dream had finally come true. But the pick was not free from criticism. After all, the mighty Vikings already had two Pro Bowl passers in Randall Cunningham and Jeff George. The fans and critics alike questioned why Coach Dennis Green would select a quarterback in an already crowded backfield.

"I was shocked when they drafted me to tell you the truth," said Culpepper. "I mean they already had two outstanding quarterbacks. But I knew it would work out great learning from those guys. I was just so happy to finally be a part of the NFL and to be a first round draft pick. I had so much anxiety leading up to that and when I finally heard my name called by the commissioner I was just so relieved to have it over with. Overall though, I was really happy to be coming to Minnesota. I knew about the great tradition that they had here and I was excited to be a part of it."

In a press conference following the draft, Coach Green said that Culpepper was the best player available at that

Minnesota Vikings Head Coach Dennis Green said that he drafted Daunte Culpepper because he believed that Culpepper represented a new generation of bigger and more athletic quarterbacks.

point, and it would have been foolish to simply pass on him. He knew that Cunningham and George were veterans getting up there in years and thought that Culpepper would be a perfect fit to learn the playbook first hand under their tutelage. So many of the young quarterbacks in the league were being thrown into the starting lineup and did not have the necessary time to learn their systems. Culpepper, on the other hand, would now get that chance to sit a year or two and learn the proper way. It would be a great situation for Culpepper, to sit back and learn without all the pressure of having to succeed immediately.

"As a quarterback you're not ready to play as a rookie," said Coach Green. "When we drafted Daunte, we told him, 'This is the perfect situation for you. You are the only quarterback in this draft who's going to be given a chance to watch. They all think they're ready to play, but they're not.'"

Green knew what he was doing. After all, it was just a year earlier that he took a chance on another small college kid by the name of Randy Moss. The coach figured that the young wide receiver would thrive under the direction of stars like Cris Carter and Jake Reed, and he was right on the money. He now believed that lightning would strike twice in Minnesota, and as a result, his Vikings would be well on their way to the Super Bowl.

Culpepper could hardly wait to get to Minnesota and meet his new teammates. He wanted to hit the field immediately and start to learn his plays. He was ready. But first he had to sign a contract, and for that Culpepper hired the minority-owned firm of Strickland & Ashe to represent him. He wanted to get his contract done quickly, and when it was all said and done, he had signed a whopping five-year contract that included a $5 million signing bonus. The first thing he did with his new-found wealth was buy Emma a new home in a very nice neighborhood in Florida.

"I could never repay her for all that she has done for me," said Culpepper. "I was just so happy that I could do something that would make a difference in her life. She had worked so hard to take care of so many people, and it felt great to know that now I could take care of her for the rest of her life."

With his new contract signed, sealed, and delivered, Culpepper headed north, to Minneapolis, to begin his career with the Vikings. That summer, in training camp, he memorized the team's playbook and quickly became friends with the players. He asked a lot of questions and studied hard both on and off the field. He watched countless hours of game film and tried to learn as much as humanly possible. The pace was much faster in the big leagues, but Culpepper knew that when the time came, he would be ready.

The Vikings were coming off of a spectacular 15–1 record in 1998 and were the odds-on favorites to win the Super Bowl. Led by their Pro Bowl running back Robert Smith and their "three-deep" wide receiver trio of Randy Moss, Cris Carter, and Jake Reed, their offense was the most potent in the entire NFL. The team got off to a shaky start that season though, going 2–4 before rebounding to get back into the playoff race. Midway through the season Coach Green, knowing that he needed to shake things up a bit, replaced Cunningham with George. It worked. The offense immediately began to show signs of life, and after a 40–16 win over the San Francisco 49ers, the Vikes were back in the Super Bowl hunt.

That game was also a pivotal one for Culpepper, who got to see his first NFL action during the fourth quarter. Culpepper came in while the team was way ahead and actually looked pretty good. He took just six snaps, attempted no passes, but did convert a key first down on a nice 9-yard run. He did, however, mess up a simple kneel-down play at the end of the game, but at that point no

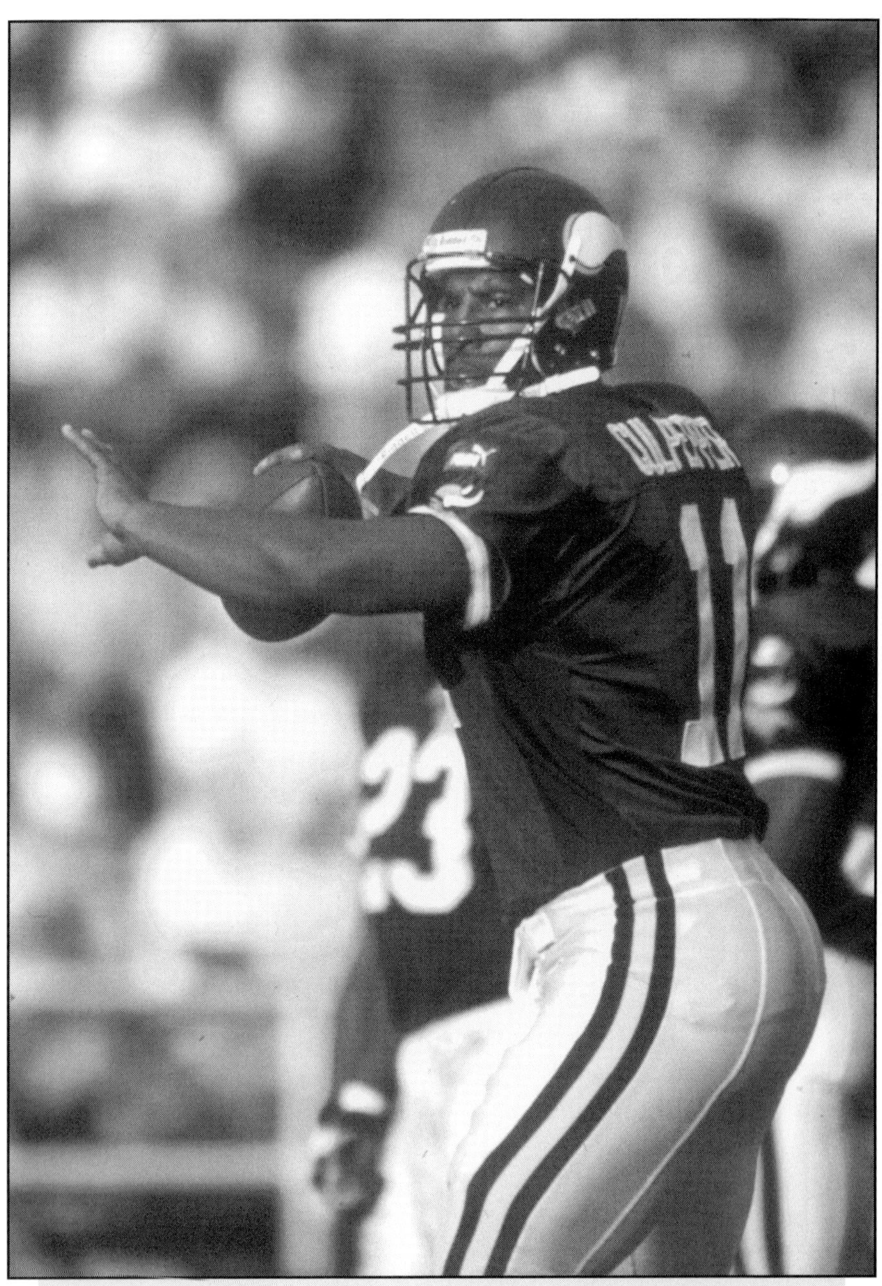

Daunte Culpepper saw his first NFL game action against the San Francisco 49ers midway through his rookie season.

one really cared. The Vikes had won the contest and would roll on to win seven of their final nine games to make the playoffs.

The team ultimately lost to the Rams early in the post-season, but Culpepper had a great year of learning under his belt. Sure, he had only gotten into one game, but he knew that the next season would be different. He watched several of the other first-round QBs struggle in their starts, and he knew that he was in a good situation by being able to watch and learn.

"Looking at the big picture I guess it was a good thing that I had a year to sit back and learn the system under a pair of great quarterbacks," said Culpepper. "But for me personally, I would have much rather been out on the field. I mean I am a competitor and to sit on the sidelines makes me crazy. I was so anxious to get out there but I knew that I would be a better all-around player if I absorbed it all from Jeff (George) and Randall (Cunningham). I had to learn patience though, and that was something new to me."

Chapter 5

Rising Star

That off-season Culpepper worked out and studied even harder. He knew that his sophomore campaign would be an important one and he wanted to be ready. Then, something happened that would forever change Daunte Culpepper's life. Both of Minnesota's Pro Bowl quarterbacks, Jeff George and Randall Cunningham, decided to sign contracts with new teams. The Vikings did not have as much money under the league-imposed salary cap that many of the other teams did, and decided that they could part ways with them. So, after an unsuccessful attempt to woo future Hall of Fame quarterback Dan Marino out of retirement, the team figured no time was better than the present for a youth movement. As a result, Culpepper was suddenly thrust into the starting lineup for the home opener against the Chicago Bears. Green did, however, sign former Denver Broncos QB Bubby Brister, a seasoned veteran, as the team's back-up.

"I have full confidence in Coach Green," said Culpepper of his decision to name him as the starter. "He's been successful year in and year out and he knows what it takes to get the job done. I would have loved to work with Dan Marino, he's a Hall of Famer, let's face it. But, on the other hand, we have Bubby Brister, who's had some great seasons as well. He's a great guy and I think we're going to work well together."

When the news of Coach Green's decision to go with Culpepper hit the airwaves, the media went crazy. Talk-radio stations throughout Minnesota were filled with nothing but talk of the Vikings and just what they were thinking by going with an unproven kid who, up until that point, had not even thrown a pass in the NFL. Green, who had taken a lot of criticism from the fans for drafting Culpepper instead of Rookie of the Year Jevon Kearse, was now in the hot-seat. He did not care though. He had made his choice to go with Culpepper. He knew that Culpepper was going to be something special. Culpepper was ecstatic.

Culpepper came out confident during the team's pre-season minicamp. His teammates quickly saw that he was more than capable of leading the offense down the field. The fans showed up in droves to the team's Mankato, Minnesota, training camp facility to catch a glimpse of their future quarterback, and before long kids throughout the Land of 10,000 Lakes were wearing purple Daunte Culpepper jerseys.

But, how would he do in that first regular season game against the Bears, when it really counted? Daunte Culpepper did not disappoint. He ran for a team record three touch-downs en route to leading the Vikes to a spectacular 30–27 come-from-behind victory.

Sure, it was just one game under his belt, but Culpepper was feeling confident. As for Coach Green, he was now looking like a genius. But that was just one game and the rest of the season was going to be a battle. The Vikings had lost several key free agents that off-season, including a couple of Pro Bowl offensive linemen in Jeff Christy and Randall McDaniel. Culpepper still had Cris Carter, Randy

Moss, and Robert Smith though, a backfield that many felt was the most potent in all of football.

"Those guys are great," said Culpepper of his backfield teammates. "They are all Pro Bowlers and it is a real privilege to be able to play with them. They are just great competitors and that pushes me to be a better [player]."

In Week Two Culpepper faced the Miami Dolphins and their rock-solid defense. The inexperienced quarterback got rattled early in this one, as his team committed five turnovers, including an interception late in the fourth quarter. He remained calm, though, and marched his club down inside the red zone. There, he dropped back and found Randy Moss in the corner of the end zone for the game-winning touchdown.

"I really believe Daunte Culpepper and Randy Moss are going to set the league on fire," said Coach Green. "They'll do this because Daunte can throw a beautiful deep ball and because Randy has the speed to run out there and get it."

Culpepper came up big again the next week against the New England Patriots, where he completed 20 of 28 passes for three touchdowns in a 21–13 win. Very quietly, Culpepper was earning the respect of his teammates.

"I think Daunte's poise is very good," said Randy Moss. "To my eyes, he's gaining our confidence. I've said time and time again, Daunte is the man. He's driving this boat."

After the team's bye week, the Vikes went on to rattle off three more big wins against division opponents. Culpepper found Moss on a pair of spectacular 50– and 61–yard bombs in a 31–24 win over Detroit, and then came back to toss three touchdowns in a dramatic 30–23 Monday night win over the Tampa Bay Buccaneers in Game Five. All Culpepper did in this one was orchestrate a 73–yard, come-from-behind fourth-quarter drive that ended with a 42–yard game-winning TD pass to Moss. The next week

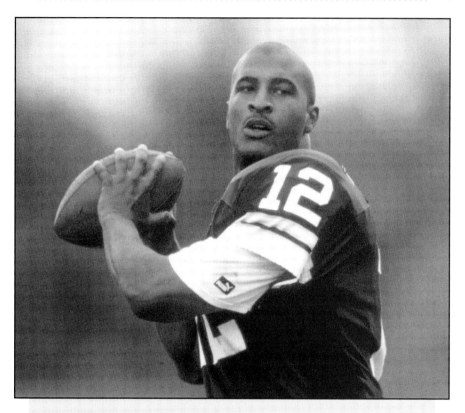

Before the start of his second year in the NFL, the Minnesota Vikings announced that Daunte Culpepper would be the team's new starting quarterback.

Daunte again tossed a trio of TDs, this time to make it a clean sweep over the Bears in the Windy City, 28–16.

Through six games, Minnesota was undefeated and Culpepper was among the top-rated passers in the NFL. He had tossed 11 touchdown passes to only six picks and was averaging 5.0 yards per carry.

"What he's done is help us win," said Coach Green. "That's the number one job of a starting quarterback. Daunte will do what he needs to for success. If you look at each game, each game is a little bit different. A lot of it is based on what the defense is going to give you, and Daunte is always willing to do what it's going to take for the offense to score. If it's all passing and no running, that's fine with him."

Culpepper heaved three more touchdowns to defeat the Buffalo Bills in Week Seven, keeping their undefeated season going strong. With the season nearly halfway over, the Vikes were already thinking playoffs. Some speculated that with Culpepper, Moss, and Carter hitting on all cylinders, no one could beat this club.

But the team's defense was struggling and that was something Culpepper could not do anything about. All he could do was focus on scoring as many points as possible in order to give the team its best shot at winning. That next week, Culpepper, despite throwing for 276 yards and a pair of touchdowns, also tossed three interceptions as the Vikes lost a 26–20 overtime heart-breaker in Green Bay. From there it was three more touchdowns in a win over Arizona, followed by a 31–17 pounding of Carolina. Culpepper posted a career-high 357 yards passing that afternoon, going 22-of-29 with another trio of TDs.

The following week the team got a big dose of exposure when they defeated the Dallas Cowboys in front of a nationally televised Thanksgiving day audience. Culpepper tossed two touchdowns that day as the Vikes rolled to a 27–15 victory. After beating Detroit that next weekend, the Purple got a reality check against the high-powered St. Louis Rams. Despite Culpepper's three touchdown passes and one TD run, Kurt Warner, Marshall Faulk, and Isaac Bruce each contributed in the Ram's 40–29 pounding—giving Minnesota fans reason to be concerned about their soft defense.

From there the Vikes hit the skids, falling to Green Bay and Indianapolis to round out the season on a downer. Against the Packers, Culpepper threw a career-long 78-yard

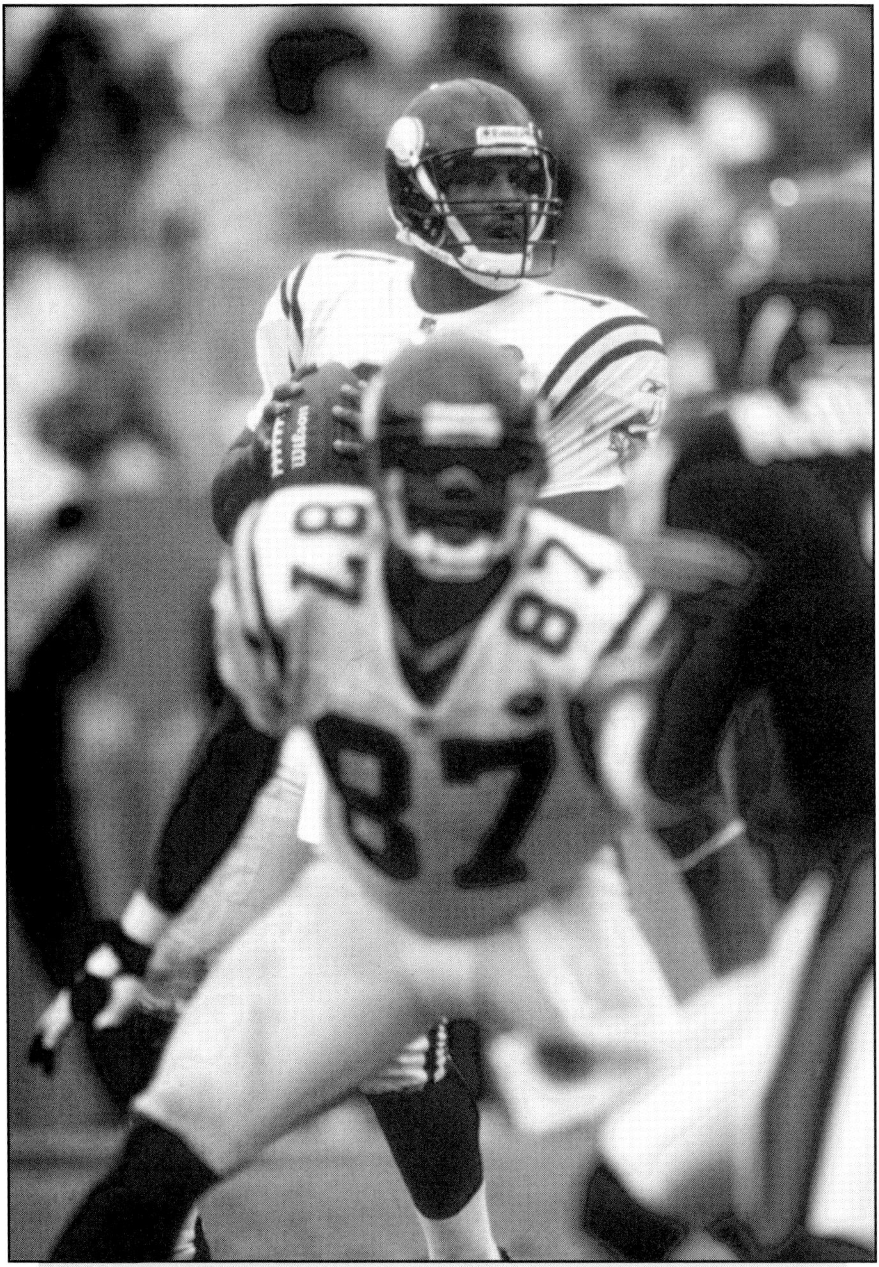

Culpepper drops back to pass while his offensive line tries to hold back the opposing defense.

touchdown pass to Randy Moss, despite suffering a high ankle sprain. He came back to start at Indianapolis in the regular season finale, but left in the first quarter when he re-aggravated the injury. Backup QB Bubby Brister came in for mop-up duty but the Vikes got hammered, 31–10.

When Minnesota lost those final three games of the year, many speculated that there was no way this team could win the Super Bowl. Culpepper did not care, though. Sure, the team had limped into the post-season, but they were ready to make a playoff run and that was all that mattered.

Because the team had won the Central Division crown and had the best record in their division, they had earned a first-round playoff bye. The much-needed rest proved to be invaluable, as the team collected itself for its upcoming matchup against the red-hot New Orleans Saints, who had just beaten the heavily favored Rams in the NFC Wild Card game.

Culpepper was eager to show the world that he and his Vikings were for real. The Saints, who were without their star running back, Ricky Williams, still had a lot of offensive weapons. Plus, their defense was rock-solid—something that was going to be difficult for Culpepper to overcome. Minnesota came out running and gunning, though, in front of a Metrodome crowd that was primed and ready for action. How would the rookie quarterback do in his first-ever playoff game? He came out and showed no signs of trouble from his ankle sprain, throwing for 302 yards and three touchdowns, including touchdown passes of 53 and 68 yards to Randy Moss, leading his Vikes to a convincing 34–16 win.

Minnesota was just one victory away from the Super Bowl. It was now off to the Big Apple to face the New York Giants in the NFC Championship Game.

On January 14th, 2001, the Vikings entered Giants Stadium just sixty minutes away from the promised land of

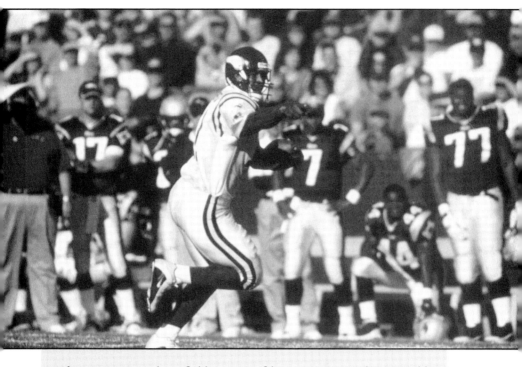

Culpepper points downfield to one of his receivers as he scrambles outside the pocket.

Miami, Florida, the home of Super Bowl XXXV. The Minnesota fans were hungry for a championship. Just two years earlier they had gotten upset by the Atlanta Falcons in the NFC Championship Game on a heart-breaking overtime field goal. Going back to the 1970s, Minnesota had met defeat in four Super Bowls. Fans knew that the Vikings needed to play solid, two-way football to have a chance against the Giants.

New York came out and scored 14 points before the Vikings even knew what hit them. Minnesota could not get to Giants quarterback Kerry Collins, and he made them pay. He threw short, he threw long, and he pounded the Vikings at every turn. The Giants could do no wrong.

Culpepper, on the other hand, could do no right. He completed just 13 passes, threw three interceptions, and—for the first time ever—got shut out in a game. The Giants ended up winning, 41–0.

"That was one of the worst experiences I have ever had on the football field," said Culpepper. "It was probably the worst feeling I have ever had in sports. I mean I have been playing football since I was a little kid, and not once have I ever been shut out like that. That was really tough on me, and it is something that will stay with me forever. What it did do, however, was show me what can happen when you are not prepared. We just got behind and couldn't get back on track. They had it all working for them [and] we just couldn't get it in gear. I learned a lot about myself though, and I know that I will be a better player in the future because of it."

Despite the loss, all in all it was an outstanding season for Culpepper. He finished the year with a quarterback rating of 98.0 as he threw for 3,937 yards and 33 touchdowns. In addition, he completed 62.7 percent of his passes, and also ran for 470 yards while rushing for seven more touchdowns. He also became just the fifth quarterback in NFL history to post 40 combined rushing/receiving touchdowns in a season, joining Dan Marino, Steve Young, Kurt Warner, and Brett Favre.

When it was all said and done, he was tabbed as the NFC's starting quarterback in the Pro Bowl that January in Hawaii. It would be a sweet reward for an outstanding season.

Chapter 6

Daunte's Inferno

That off-season Culpepper took some time to reflect on what went wrong. He was determined not to let the New York game get the best of him. He worked hard and vowed to come to training camp in even better mental and physical condition. He knew it was going to take a lot of dedication and sacrifice to become a champion, but he was ready for the challenge.

"I've been watching a lot of film this off season," said Culpepper. "We've been meeting every morning, working with new guys and we've got some new faces around here. And it's just motivating me and keeping the tempo of practice. I think that's been a big part of my stepping up more as a leader. I think that's been a big part of me getting better and me becoming a better quarterback in this offense."

The previous season he threw the ball short, threw it deep, and ran over would-be defenders. This season he would be asked to do even more. And, he would be asked to do it without several of the starters from the squad that made it all the way to the NFC title game. Overall, he was realistic about the past and optimistic about the future.

"It happens like that sometimes," Culpepper said of the loss to the Giants. "Never ever like that before in my career, and, hopefully, it never happens again. But you're going to have those days. Unluckily for us, it was the NFC Championship Game, the most important game in my life so far. To get that close and to not get what you want to get is tough. But at the same time, you have to look at the whole season and say, 'It was a good year.' All we can do is regroup now. As soon as that game was over, I was just thinking about next season. I was thinking about this off-season, preparing myself and the rest of the team, and getting ready. That was my focus."

When the team came together that following August for training camp, there were a lot of new faces. There were also a lot of old faces that were missing, particularly that of Pro Bowler Robert Smith, who unexpectedly decided to retire. Several other key members of the team also defected via free agency, most notably Pro Bowl defensive tackle John Randle, who signed with the Seattle Seahawks. The team drafted first round pick Michael Bennett from the University of Wisconsin to replace Smith, but overall, the general attitude of the team was down.

Culpepper knew his role and was ready to step up and become a team leader. He was not a screamer; rather, he was a "lead-by-example" type of leader and wanted to quietly gain his teammates' respect.

"I look at it like, when the season starts, practice should be hard, games should be easy," he said. "I expect to be the same type of quarterback I was this past season—efficient. Go out there and look smooth. Run the offense like it should be run. Like Coach Green says, the offense is like a car and I'm just the driver. I do my part. I drive the car."

"I think Daunte goes into the 2001 season with even more determination," added Coach Green. "He has the discipline that says that the things that you want in life, you have to work to achieve—that nothing comes easy. He's

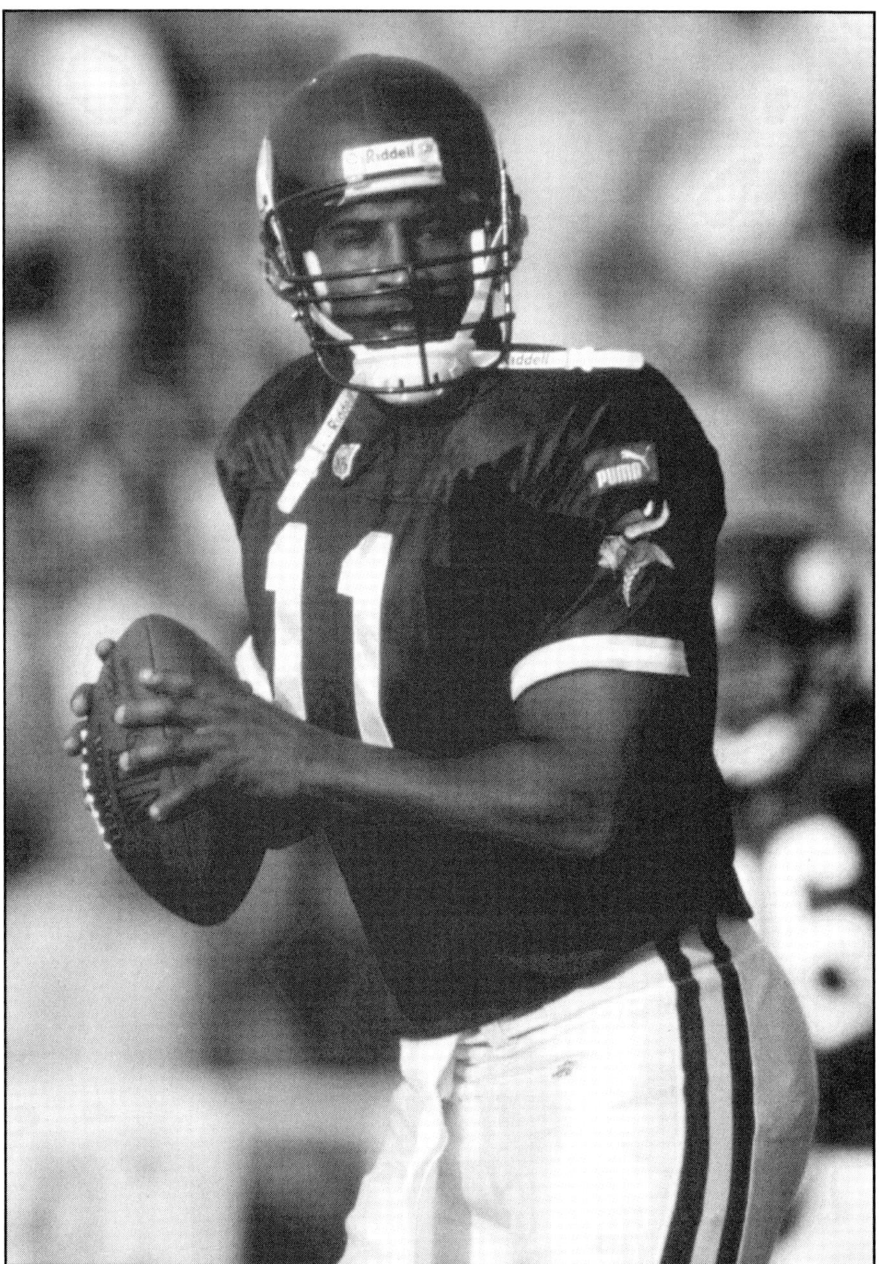

As the 2001 season approached, Daunte Culpepper began to assume a greater leadership role with the Vikings.

always been able to deal with disappointment and come back from it."

Despite all of the off-season turmoil and the players' efforts to overcome their emotions, the most significant thing to happen to this team came just days into training camp. That's when All-Pro offensive tackle Korey Stringer collapsed due to heat exhaustion during practice one afternoon and died. The temperature was well above 100 degrees that day and "Big K," as he was affectionately known, had wanted to work as hard as possible to get himself into game shape. The entire team was devastated.

The team took a few days off for Korey Stringer's funeral and then tried to regroup. It was impossible, though. Stringer, arguably the most liked and well-respected player on the team, was too good of a friend to the players for them to simply get back to work like nothing had happened. The team did go undefeated in its four exhibition games—leading many to believe that Stringer's death would rally the team together in victory—but when the season got underway, things quickly fell apart.

The opening play of the 2001 season was probably a good indicator of what was in store for the club. It came at home, against the lowly Carolina Panthers, when Steve Smith took the opening kickoff 93 yards for a touchdown, leaving the 65,000 Metrodome fans speechless. The game got ugly from there as Culpepper, despite completing 22 of 38 passes for 236 yards and throwing one touchdown while running for another, looked shaky. He tied his career high with three interceptions, and could not jump-start a tired looking Minnesota offense. The result: a 24–13 home-opening defeat.

What happened next was something no one ever could have expected. As the team got ready to play the Baltimore Ravens in Week Two, the unbelievable events of September 11, 2001, unfolded in New York City and

Washington, D.C. As a result, sports across America came to a screeching halt and all the games were postponed. Players just wanted to get home to be with their families. Football was the furthest thing from anyone's mind.

When the NFL resumed action on September 23rd, the Vikings traveled to Chicago, to play the Bears. After a very emotional pre-game Star-Spangled Banner, the players came out and tried to do their best to play a game under these extraordinary conditions. There, in front of 66,944 rain-soaked fans at Soldier Field, the Bears defeated the Vikes, 17–10. The Vikings had dropped to 0–2 for the first time since 1984, and things were not looking good. There were too many penalties, too many turnovers, too many special-teams breakdowns, and too few ways for the offense to score.

The team rebounded the following week to beat rival Tampa Bay at home, 20–16, to finally get a "W." Culpepper, who threw for 322 yards in the game, completed six consecutive passes at the end of this one to cap a thrilling 96-yard touchdown drive with an 8-yard run to put Minnesota ahead for good.

"Daunte Culpepper is something special," said renowned football analyst John Madden. "He can throw the ball and do all of those other things, but he is so strong that you can break one or even two pass rushers free on him and he can still complete the ball—even when you get him. You can be hanging on him and he's still strong enough to complete passes. There was one play where he had two defensive linemen hanging on him and he completed the pass. He just did that the whole game."

The euphoria did not last long, however, as the Vikes self-destructed that next week in a 28–15 loss to the New Orleans Saints. The Saints, perhaps getting a little revenge over their playoff loss at Minnesota the previous season, came out strong. The Vikings turned the ball over three times, including a fumble that was returned for a touchdown. Culpepper was sacked three times and tossed one interception in the game.

"It's tough when they've got a front four like they've got," Culpepper said of the Saints' defense. "They just put the pressure on me, and I couldn't really find anything but underneath routes."

From there Minnesota scratched back to .500 with victories over Detroit and Green Bay. Against the Lions, Culpepper threw for 244 yards and a touchdown to Carter, while also leading the team with 83 yards rushing and a pair of TDs on the ground. Against the Packers, Culpepper completed 18 of 27 passes for 184 yards, including 43 on another touchdown to Carter. Once again, Culpepper was a force to be reckoned with on the ground, this time rushing for 71 yards and yet another touchdown.

After evening their record at 3–3, the Vikes went through an ugly stretch, losing big to both Tampa Bay, 41–14, and Philadelphia, 48–17. The team's defense was getting pounded and the players were getting frustrated. In the Tampa Bay game, Culpepper proved how tough he was, though, playing through a broken nose that he suffered early in the first quarter. Then, in the Philly game, Culpepper lost two fumbles, threw an interception, and was sacked six times.

"Offensively, we have to learn to play better when things are going bad," he said. "We can't just play good when things are going good."

The team did rebound to beat those same Giants who had humiliated them in the 2000 NFC Championship game, but then lost six of their final seven games to finish their season. In the 13–6 loss to Chicago that following week, Culpepper hurt his knee. At first it seemed like just a sprain, but after the game the doctors saw that it was much worse. He played that next week in a 21–16 loss to Pittsburgh, but when Coach Green saw him limping on the field, he was replaced with backup QB Todd Bouman.

Culpepper, who had never missed a game due to injury, was suddenly on the outside looking in. It would be a sad ending to a sad season. From Big K's untimely death in training camp to the tragic events of September 11th, this campaign seemed to be doomed from the onset.

Bouman, a Minnesota native and fan favorite, came in and rallied the Vikings to a big 42–24 win that next week over Tennessee. The fans were feeling good about their back-up insurance policy, but the honeymoon ended when Bouman got hurt that next week and had to be replaced with the team's third-string quarterback, Spergon Wynn. From there it got even uglier. Detroit, a team which had not won a game all year, beat the Vikes 27–24. This was followed by consecutive defeats at the hands of Green Bay and Baltimore to round out Minnesota's dismal season. There would be no playoff party this year.

Culpepper hung in there and offered his support to the backups. He wanted to be the ultimate team player and help his club any way he could, even though it was killing him not to be out there competing.

"That was one of the toughest things I have gone through, to miss a game," said Culpepper. "Watching that first game that next week was miserable. I had a migraine headache while I was watching on TV, and I was just beside myself. It was so tough to not be in there. I was so frustrated but I knew that I would be back that next season even stronger."

The 2002 off-season was a real changing of the guard in Minnesota. The biggest shocker came after the season when long-time head coach Dennis Green was let go by team owner Red McCombs and was replaced by assistant head coach and former Viking tight end Mike Tice. In addition, Cris Carter, the team's all-time leading scorer and

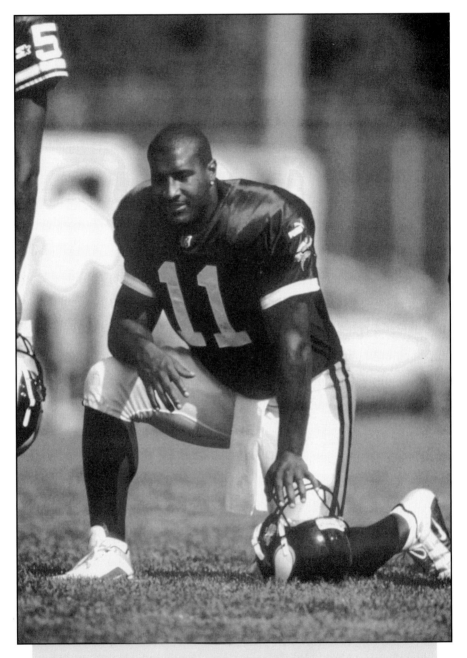

A knee injury in late 2001 forced Culpepper out of action for the first time in his football career.

future Hall of Famer, decided to leave via free agency, as did several other key players.

Culpepper understood that this was a business and that losing key players was just a part of the game. He did not like it, but knew that it was not personal. He vowed to keep working hard and to one day bring a championship to the fans of Minnesota.

At six-foot-four and 260 pounds, Daunte Culpepper has truly redefined the position of quarterback. He is arguably the game's most versatile and respected offensive threat and, incredibly, he is really still several years away from being in the prime of his career.

In addition, Culpepper has become an outstanding role model and citizen in his community. Among the numerous charities that he donates his time to are the African American Adoption Agency and Permanency Placement, on which he serves as the national spokesperson. Culpepper and his wife Kimberly have four kids of their own, but Culpepper has said that they may adopt another child in the future as well.

"I wouldn't be here today if it weren't for adoption, so I am very grateful for that," he said. "Who knows, maybe one day we will be able to give a little kid the same opportunity that I was blessed with, that would be pretty amazing."

For now, Culpepper has his head on straight and is focused on being a team player. He knows that big egos do not go over really well in the locker room or with the fans. If all goes as planned, after the 2003 season he will be set to sign a new contract with the Vikings.

"I'm not worried about the money thing, that will take care of itself," said Culpepper. "My main goal is to win a Super Bowl. That is why I am here and that is what I am focused on doing. It is not my only goal though. I want to be a successful, well-rounded person too. I also want to be a great dad, teammate, and someday a great coach."

Culpepper has also embraced the Minnesota fans. Some athletes have been reluctant to come to Minnesota because of the cold weather, but not Daunte Culpepper. Being from Florida, it was certainly an adjustment, but he has made the most of it and the fans have appreciated it. Culpepper understands the Viking's rich history and is honestly humbled to be a part of it.

"Being a Viking makes me feel very proud," he said. "All of the great players—the Alan Pages, Carl Ellers, Jim Marshalls, and Ahmad Rashads—to play in the same organization as them means a lot to me. Man, those guys played in the cold back then too, outside at old Met Stadium. That just takes a special player to be able to play tough out in the elements like that. Knowing the history and tradition of the team, it just inspires me to go out and try to be the best player that I can be, and to represent the organization proudly.

"The fans are great up there," he added. "They are real die-hards and I respect that. They have so much support for the team and that makes us as players try hard to get them victories. They really show me their appreciation and for that I am very grateful. Overall they have been very respectful to me and my family and have welcomed us with open arms. Everyone is so nice and that makes it a very fun place to live and work. I just want to show them my appreciation by being the best I can be."

In addition to his fans, Daunte Culpepper also has a very loving family, which offers him a lot of much-needed support—particularly while he is up in Minnesota and they are in Florida, where they reside year-round. No matter what, though, Culpepper is always just a phone call away from his mom, a woman he simply adores.

"Mom and I talk all the time," said Culpepper. "She calls me a lot to check up on me and see how I am doing. She was really concerned about my knee surgery in 2001 and

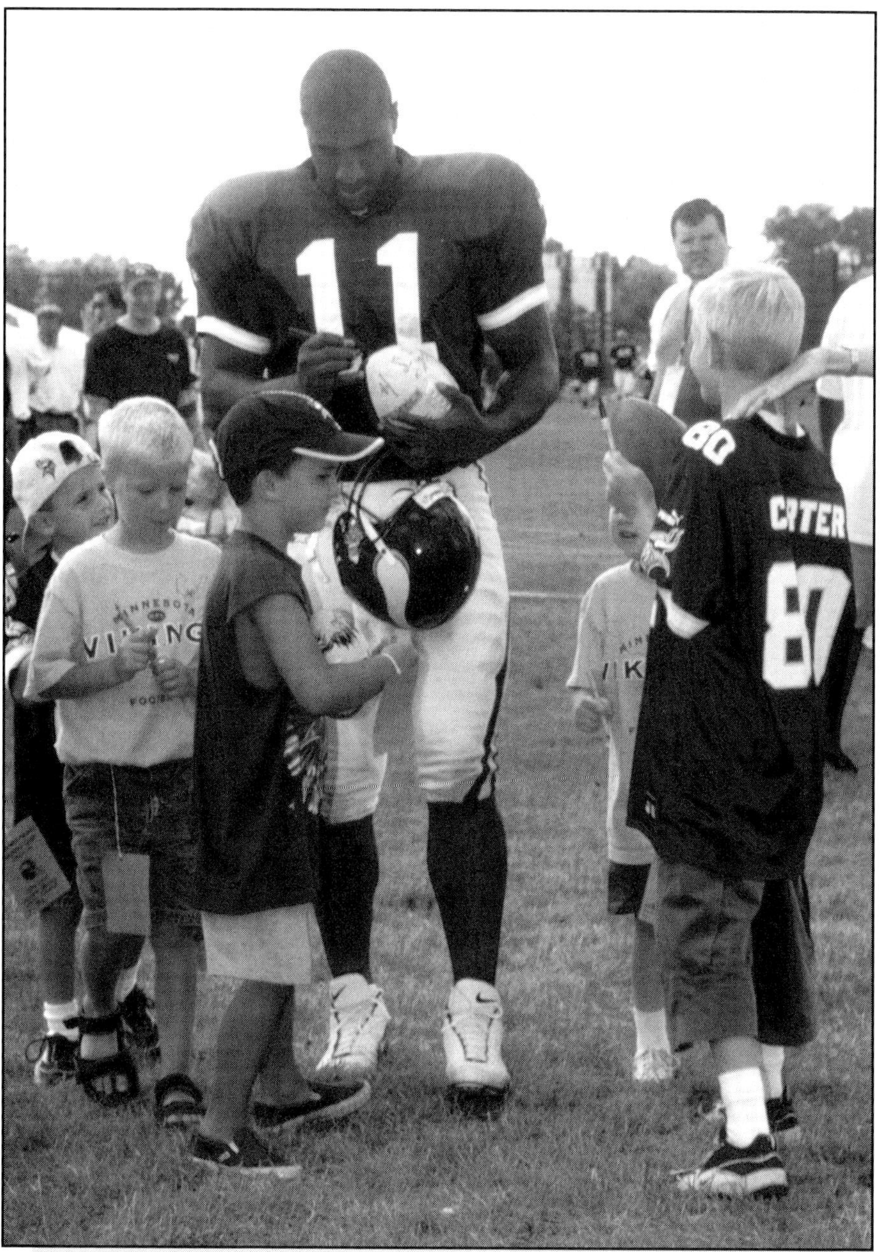

In addition to his accomplishments on the football field, Culpepper has accomplished a great deal off the field, donating his time and efforts to several charities.

keeps telling me not to push it too hard and to take it easy. She is a real worry-wart, but that is a good thing because she cares so much about me and I love that. She has done so much for me and I am so grateful to have her in my life. She is definitely my hero. Maybe I did not realize it earlier in my life but now, when I look back, I would have to say that she was the person that I looked up to and admired the most in my life. She worked so hard to make my life better and I will never, ever be able to repay her for that. She is really an amazing person and a big part of who I am today."

Even with all of his recent fame and fortune Daunte Culpepper has not forgotten who he is and where he came from. His loyalty and humility have made him a truly amazing person who kids everywhere can look up to and be proud of. Perhaps future Hall of Famer Cris Carter put it best: "Tremendous player, tremendous attitude. He's handled everything thrown at him. With the right supporting cast and staying healthy, he can be as good as anyone playing the game."

"I want to be the best ever," Culpepper said. "I don't want to be just somebody who played the game. I know that's saying a lot but I'm saying it anyway. You've got to set your goals that high. If you don't, why are you playing? The best ever . . . that's what I'm after."

Career Statistics

College

Year	Team	Games	Att	Comp	Pct	Yds	Td	Int
1995	University of Central Florida	11	294	168	57.1	2,071	12	10
1996	University of Central Florida	11	314	187	59.6	2,565	19	15
1997	University of Central Florida	11	381	238	62.5	3,086	25	10
1998	University of Central Florida	11	402	296	73.6	3,690	28	7
Totals		44	1,391	889	63.9	11,412	84	42

NFL

Year	Team	Games	Att	Comp	Pct	Yds	Td	Int
1999	Minnesota	1	0	0	0.0	0	0	0
2000	Minnesota	16	474	297	62.7	3,937	33	16
2001	Minnesota	11	366	235	64.2	2,612	14	13
2002	Minnesota	16	549	333	60.7	3,853	18	23
Totals		44	1,389	865	62.3	10,402	65	52

Att = Attempts
Comp = Completions
Pct = Completion Percentage
Yds = Yards
Td = Touchdowns
Int = Interceptions

Where to Write Daunte Culpepper

Mr. Daunte Culpepper
c/o The Minnesota Vikings
9520 Viking Drive
Eden Prairie, MN 55344

On the Internet at:

http://www.nfl.com
http://www.vikings.com

Index